'Or, as I call it – Brexit'

THE BEST OF

MATT

2016

MATTHEW PRITCHETT
studied at St Martin's School of Art in
London and first saw himself published
in the *New Statesman* during one of its
rare lapses from high seriousness. He has
been the *Daily Telegraph*'s front-page
pocket cartoonist since 1988. In 1995,
1996, 1999, 2005, 2009 and 2013 he
was the winner of the Cartoon Arts Trust
Award and in 1991, 2004 and 2006 he
was 'What the Papers Say' Cartoonist of
the Year. In 1996, 1998, 2000, 2008 and
2009 he was the *UK Press Gazette*
Cartoonist of the Year and in 2015 he
was awarded the Journalist's Charity
Award. In 2002 he received an MBE.

The Daily Telegraph

THE BEST OF

MATT

2016

An Orion Paperback

First published in Great Britain in 2016 by Orion Books
A division of the Orion Publishing Group Ltd
Carmelite House
50 Victoria Embankment
London
EC4Y 0DZ

An Hachette UK Company

10 9 8 7 6 5 4 3 2 1

A CIP catalogue record for this book is available from the British Library.

ISBN: 978 1 4091 4836 4

Printed in the UK by CPI Group (UK) Ltd, Croydon, CR0 4YY.

The Orion Publishing Group's policy is to use papers that are natural,
renewable and recyclable products and made from wood grown in
sustainable forests. The logging and manufacturing processes are
expected to conform to the environmental regulations of the country
of origin.

www.orionbooks.co.uk

'And this little piggy
grew a pancreas for
human transplant'

THE BEST OF
MATT
2016

'We can't BLAME Europe
if we're not IN Europe'

'Don't leave. You'll be poorer,
have less influence and it
might lead to war in Europe'

'I feel the wording of the
question "Do you take this
man ...?" is biased towards
an "I do" outcome'

'It's an EU themed restaurant.
We don't tell them what
we want and they don't
give it to us'

'I used to be involved in EU
negotiations, but I found
them too stage-managed
and artificial'

'I'm an EU genie. I grant
you wishes that may
be watered down
or vetoed'

Cameron's EU Renegotiation

'Exquisitely crafted
chocolates with mildly
disappointing centres'

'I'm leaving you for
someone on a rival leave
Europe campaign'

'When you asked whether I'm an "Innie" or "Outie" were you talking about Europe or belly buttons?'

'If we sneak onto a lorry we can get out of the country for the referendum'

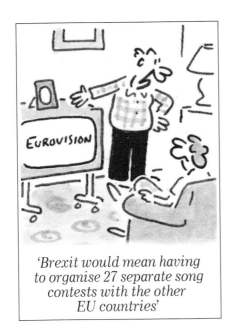

'Brexit would mean having
to organise 27 separate song
contests with the other
EU countries'

'Ignore that. It's just
scaremongering'

'Sorry. While you were out
we were able to deliver the
Government's EU leaflet'

'Trapped for seven hours,
but I never got round to
reading the EU leaflet'

'We don't need to be part of
a failing EU, we're big
enough to fail on our own'

'They say it's about dinner
money, but it's really
about Europe'

'We think King Harold might have been anti-EU'

'I can't divulge my sources, but I happen to know the Queen hates poodles'

'The PM said if you
could hit Boris it
would be appreciated'

'After President Obama has
spoken about Brexit, Prince
Philip will say a few words
about Donald Trump'

'Don't worry. Even if
we leave the EU we can
still come and enjoy
the delights of France'

'If it hadn't been for these
EU directives in my breast
pocket, the bullet would have
gone straight through my heart'

'It's my new
Telegraph T-shirt'

'At the last election he was
a Shy Tory and now he's a
Bashful Leaver'

'When this is over we must
both try and go back to
arguing about parking
spaces and noisy parties'

'We drill under the Commons
pump in high pressure water
and force out all the Brexiteers'

'There'll be an alcohol ban,
riot police and tear gas. Some
Tory nutters will be looking
for trouble on Friday'

'GET IT BACK!
I've changed my mind again'

'Let's never ask the public for their views ever again'

'Good evening. Aliens didn't land on earth and Elvis wasn't found alive, but everything else happened . . .'

Surprise Brexit vote causes chaos

'I think we should go to Britain
to give Mr Cameron a hug'

'We need migrants to do the
jobs Brits won't or can't do.
Like Prime Minister or
Leader of the Opposition'

'Thank you for resigning from the shadow cabinet. Unfortunately you've called at a particularly busy time and you're being held in a queue ...'

'It's very humane. We trap Jeremy, take him to a north London rally and release him into his natural habitat'

Pound plummets

'My father fought in the
Tory leadership election.
He never speaks of the
things he saw'

'I'm studying politics.
The course covers the period
from 8am on Thursday to
lunchtime on Friday'

Tory leadership contest turns nasty

'If May and Leadsom are
vying to be the new Maggie,
we need to know how much
their husbands can drink'

'Only men can be members
here. A woman's place is
running the country'

'At least the England footballers had a plan for leaving the EU'

'We couldn't get our son into a comprehensive, so he's a bog standard Etonian'

Theresa May forms new Cabinet

'That's not the pound,
that's Boris Johnson's career'

'Here comes the British
Foreign Secretary'

'I don't think the Chilcot report is the perfect holiday reading'

'We need a speedy plan for Brexit. I hear Sir John Chilcot is available'

Iraq report finally published

'It says "Corbyn" some of
the way through'

'Be careful. Mr McDonnell
might swoop down
and take your money'

Corbyn's first party conference

Corbyn

'It's a call for unity,
tied to a brick'

'I just hope Labour can breed
from their few remaining
Scottish supporters'

'We did it to annoy him'

'It's a kinder, gentler type of nuclear weapon'

Corbyn

'I'd like to join the parish council. I would be willing to push the nuclear button'

'Apparently, after a nuclear meltdown in the Labour Party, the only survivors would be a few Corbynistas'

'Usually they get so bored in the summer holidays. Luckily this year there's a nine-week Labour leadership contest'

'That's the third one this week. Maybe we should just vote for Jeremy Corbyn ...'

'We aim to limit the number of EU goals we let in to the tens of thousands'

'We think they come here for the in-work benefits'

'They swarm in, claim
expenses and take all the
country's claret'

'You may call them Hundreds
and Thousands, but I call
them Tens of Hundreds'

'If we get to the UK, we can all live in a van outside Alan Bennett's house'

'A terrorist has entered the UK. Don't worry, his shampoo and toothpaste were in a clear plastic bag'

'I'm visiting a patient. Can I use a junior doctor's parking space?'

'I think I left my banner inside you'

'You ought to go outside
and fall over while the
junior doctors are working'

'Antibiotics all round!'

'If you actually read what they put in these things, it's disgusting'

'I'd like to try one of those Dangerous Cocktail of Risks I keep hearing about'

'There's a huge black hole
in the centre and an
unpleasant aftertaste'

'*Windsor Castle took years to repair after the fire. I don't want some idiot to put 90 candles on a cake*'

'*When the Queen walks in, Jeremy Corbyn will leap from the cake and sing the National Anthem*'

'I had to taser the
computer, Sarge'

'My password has been hacked.
A cyber-jihadi group now
knows the names of our pets'

'I was fined 50p for an overdue book. It's just a revenue raising racket'

'You were persistently driving below the speed limit. Do you want us to STARVE?'

Speeding fines

'It is expensive, but we
encourage the residents
to organise jewel heists'

'Looks like the Treasury
have been here'

'I'd never eat a Russian athlete. They're so pumped full of chemicals'

'Don't take this if you're driving or if you have a £49 million sponsorship deal'

'Two notices: we've asked
to be classified as a sport
and Mrs Worthington has
failed a drugs test'

'Tory MPs should be paid
more than Labour MPs
because their battles are
more exciting to watch'

'Speeding? I'm a
Chelsea fan; it's not often
we get three points'

'I'd like to put my winnings
on Ken Livingstone to
become Chief Rabbi'

'We've found the problem.
You're looking at £18 billion
plus parts and labour'

'Darling, I have terrible
news! My VW Golf has
been deceiving me'

VW Emissions

'Drivers of electric
and hybrid cars may be
22 times more smug than
originally thought'

'We've done some tests and your emissions are 14 times more harmful than you claim'

'I think the Chief has bought a VW'

Super Injunctions

'I'd no idea WW2 was
over; but I do know the
name of the celebrity who
had the threesome'

'I keep forgetting the
name of the celebrity
we're not supposed to know'

'Apparently, if a male
human calls a female
human "stunning", she
bites his head off'

'Shall I compare thee
to a summer's day?...
No, I shan't'

Unwanted compliments

'Our electricity comes
from a Chinese power station.
If we mention the Dalai lama
the lights go out'

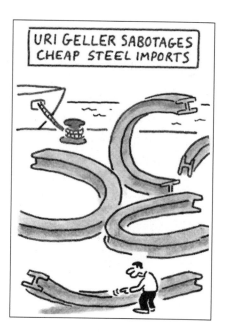

URI GELLER SABOTAGES
CHEAP STEEL IMPORTS

'Customers! Millions of them'

'Sir Philip Green thinks
"Humility" might be a
better name for his yacht'

'You say "tomaydo",
we say "tomato".
You say "Trump", we say
"Are you out of your mind?"'

'Raw or burnt? It's like
the choice between
Trump and Clinton'

'You should see the box of
fish fingers that got away'

'We're calling her Imogen
because of her terrible wind'

Storm Imogen

'So I've decided we take from the rich – except Google'

'I'm from Google. We've done a deal with the weather'

'I also hate your stupid
laugh and the noise you
make when you eat'

'I'm trying to throw it into
next door's garden'

And finally . . .

'I don't like phoning
Northumbria police.
You never know what you
might be interrupting'

Sex scandal

'I want you to pretend you're
from Hacked Off and that I'm
a naughty newspaper editor'

'We've been monitoring you on
social media, Mr Fawkes
#gunpowderplot
#Parliament #boom'

'You've been upgraded to
rear gunner. You're in charge
of shooting down drones'

And finally . . .

'Let's face it, when Prince George is at the school I'll never be Joseph in the nativity play'

Young Royals

'It's the Treasury – they say you've had enough'

'I can't come to church. The Communion wine will push me over my weekly limit'

And finally . . .

And finally . . .

'I'm going to hide this from my wife. We're going through a messy divorce'

And finally …

And finally . . .

'We've agreed to exhibit
Lady Thatcher's handbags'

'Battle of Britain?
I thought this was the
Lib Dem conference'

'I'm not a politician. I want
my tax return to be legal
but morally wrong'

'Is it for Sunday lunch
or for a debauched
university ritual?'

Cameron biography

'The arrival of Siberian swans is traditionally a sign that our boiler is about to stop working'

'The 8.45 is delayed because the women's carriage kept the rest of the train waiting'

Winter warnings

'This washing machine has many programmes: cottons, woollens, lottery tickets …'

Lost lottery ticket

'Can you take me somewhere with better phone reception, I want to order an Uber cab'

And finally . . .

'Would you gift wrap it, please – it's a present'

'A customer has sent us a complaint about our broadband service'

'The stores are closed on Sunday so I'm shopping online. What's the wi-fi password here?'

And finally . . .

'Apparently, this is
the tea room the
Russian agents visited'

Polonium poisoning

'Your pension fund fell
so dramatically that scientists
were able to detect its
gravitational waves'

'Since the election, we've
changed the way we do
opinion polls'

And finally . . .

'A second bottle? I think you've expressed enough solidarity with France this evening'

'You'd better drive. I had a liqueur chocolate in 1974'

Attacks in France

'I'm thinking of holding him back from school for a few million years'

'I'm worried he hasn't made friends at his new school. He hasn't sexted anyone'

And finally . . .

'I'm going to school,
don't wait up'

'I think our son successfully
rid the nativity play of any
Christian overtones'

'Your son's in the sick bay.
Someone spoke harshly to
him during non-contact rugby'

'I thought our son was refusing
to leave home. The UN says
we're arbitrarily detaining
him and he should be
paid compensation'

Julian Assange's claim

And finally . . .

Women banned

'Sometimes I feel like
I'm a man trapped inside
a woman's salary'